For information address
wtpublishinghouse@gmail.com

Paperback ISBN: 978-1-7388819-0-1
eBook ISBN: 978-1-7388819-1-8

Wumpus Tumpus

Gets a Puppy

Wumpus looked out the window, as he rode in the car.

His mom said they were going somewhere special, and it was rather quite far.

There were cows and horses and fields of grass, as far as Wumpus could see.

It felt like the longest drive in history!

Finally they drove up a long bumpy road, with a big red barn at the end.

Mom turned and smiled as she asked, “Are you ready to meet a new special friend?”

“I guess so”, said Wumpus. “Is he little like me?”

She grinned and replied, “Even smaller, you’ll see! He might not even come up to your knee!”

Wumpus laughed, “No way, Mom. That’s like the size of a cup!”

Then a farmer opened the barn door and out ran a pup!

He ran up to Wumpus, tail wagging so hard, that it shook the fur on his fluffy white hiney!

"You were right Mom," exclaimed Wumpus. "He is pretty tiny!"

The pup cuddled up to Wumpus, licking his face and making it gooey.

The farmer remarked, “He’s a celebrity around here, so we named him Clooney.

“He needs a new friend to
give him a home.

“Someone to feed him and walk him and brush his fur with a comb!

"Your mom says you're a good boy,
who does all his chores.

"So, if you promise to take care of him, then he is all yours!"

“You mean it?” asked
Wumpus, “I promise, I do!

“I will love him forever and
keep him safe and happy
too!”

And with that they said their goodbyes and headed back down the road.

In the back of the car, Clooney and
Wumpus were so tired and it
showed.

As they drifted to sleep,
they began sawing logs.

Mom chuckled to herself,
"Just a boy and his dog."

Manufactured by Amazon.ca
Bolton, ON

32447699R00017